T0182215

IT IS IMPOSSIBLE TO REMAIN SILENT

JORGE SEMPRÚN and ELIE WIESEL

IT IS IMPOSSIBLE TO REMAIN SILENT

Reflections on Fate and Memory in Buchenwald

Translated by **Peggy Frankston**
with an introduction by **Radu Ioanid**

Published in Association with the
United States Holocaust Memorial Museum

INDIANA UNIVERSITY PRESS

This book is a publication of
INDIANA UNIVERSITY PRESS

Office of Scholarly Publishing
Herman B Wells Library 350
1320 East 10th Street
Bloomington, Indiana 47405 USA

iupress.indiana.edu

English-language translation
© United States Holocaust Memorial Museum, 2020

Published in Association with the
United States Holocaust Memorial Museum

First published in French as *Se taire est impossible.* © Mille et une nuit, département
des éditions Fayard/Arte editions, 1995.

The assertions, arguments, and conclusions contained herein are those of the
author or other contributors. They do not necessarily reflect the opinions of the
United States Holocaust Memorial Museum.

Manufactured in the United States of America

Cataloging information is available from the Library of Congress.

ISBN 978-0-253-04528-7 (hardback)
ISBN 978-0-253-04529-4 (e-book)

1 2 3 4 5   25 24 23 22 21 20

CONTENTS

PUBLISHER'S NOTE

On March 1, 1995, during the period when the fiftieth anniversary of the liberation of the Nazi camps was being commemorated, ARTE[1] proposed an encounter between two highly regarded figures of our time, Elie Wiesel and Jorge Semprún, on its program *Entretien* (conversation).

These two men, whose destinies were unparalleled, had probably crossed paths, without ever meeting, in 1945 in the Nazi concentration camp Buchenwald.

In 1995 they met to evoke the experience they had shared, although it was different for each of them. During this encounter, they brought reflections and fundamental questions to the fore.

We felt that it was absolutely essential to make their voices heard, because if, in some sense, speaking about this subject is impossible, keeping silent should not be permitted.

Here is the entire transcription of the TV program "Conversation between Elie Wiesel and Jorge Semprún," proposed by Klaus Wenger and Laurent Andres, directed by Stéphane Loison, and broadcast on March 1, 1995.

1. The French-German state-funded television network devoted to history, the arts, and politics. It is somewhat analogous to the Public Broadcasting Service (PBS) in the United States.

IT IS IMPOSSIBLE TO REMAIN SILENT

INTRODUCTION BY RADU IOANID

About Elie Wiesel

ELIE WIESEL AND JORGE SEMPRÚN INITIALLY HAD nothing in common. But destiny brought them together.

Wiesel was born in 1928 in Sighet, Romania, to a middle-class Jewish family. He spoke Yiddish, Hungarian, and Romanian. He studied the Talmud and dreamed of becoming a learned teacher of Kabbalah. Sensitive, with an inclination to ponder existential questions, Wiesel was a delicate human being from an early age. As a child and as a teenager, he suffered the consequences of Romanian and, later, Hungarian antisemitism.

On May 16, 1944, after being marked with the yellow star and interned for twenty-six days in the local ghetto, Wiesel was deported by the Hungarian gendarmerie. Together with his family, he was included in the first transport of the Jews of Sighet sent to Auschwitz. His mother, Sarah, and younger sister, Tzipora, were gassed upon arrival in the camp. "Never shall I forget that smoke.... Never shall I forget those flames that consumed my faith forever.... Never shall I forget those moments that murdered my God and my soul and turned my dreams into ashes," Wiesel wrote in *Night*, his autobiographical account of his time in the Nazi camps.[1]

Having lied about his age, Wiesel was selected for work in Auschwitz and one of its subcamps, Monowitz. Robbed of everything—including his gold dental crown—Wiesel was put to work hauling stone blocks and loading motors onto train cars. He was beaten, starved, and forced to witness the executions of fellow inmates. He was evacuated from Auschwitz by the SS in the bitter cold of January 1945, first on foot and then in an open freight car. According to SS statistics, fifty-two inmates perished during this transport.

Encouraged by a 1954 conversation with French philosopher and Nobel Prize winner François Mauriac, Wiesel published the acclaimed autobiographical novel *Night*, first in Yiddish (1956), then in French (1958), and then in English (1960). *Night* was subsequently translated into more than thirty languages. Wiesel, who always wrote in French, authored more than sixty books and won prestigious literary awards such as the Prix Médicis. He went on to hold the Andrew W. Mellon Professorship in the Humanities at Boston University. A dedicated humanist, Wiesel strongly defended the cause of the oppressed: Soviet Jews, indigenous peoples in Nicaragua, the "disappeared" in Argentina, Kurds in Iraq, and victims of apartheid in South Africa.

Wiesel was the founding chairman of the United States Holocaust Memorial Museum in Washington, DC, and in 1986 he was awarded the Nobel Peace Prize.

About Jorge Semprún

JORGE (GEORGES) SEMPRÚN WAS BORN IN 1923 IN Madrid to a well-established liberal Catholic family. He was tutored in the fine arts and literature. His maternal grandfather, Antonio Maura, served as the prime minister of Spain more than once, and his father, José, a distinguished lawyer, represented Republican Spain as its top diplomat in the Netherlands during the Spanish Civil War. Because of this Republican allegiance, the family found itself in exile as early as 1936. In 1939, Semprún's parents sent him to study in Paris at the prestigious Lycée Henri-IV.

A member of the French communist resistance, Semprún was arrested by the Gestapo on October 8, 1943, in Joigny, France. He was imprisoned first in Auxerre, where he was tortured, and later in Dijon and the Royallieu camp in Compiègne. On January 27, 1944, he was deported as a political prisoner in a freight car to the German concentration camp Buchenwald. He was liberated at this camp on April 11, 1945.

After liberation, Semprún worked for UNESCO. Starting in 1953, he lived and worked in Madrid as a high-ranking clandestine organizer for the banned Spanish Communist Party. In 1964, he was expelled from the party for disagreeing with its sectarian leadership in exile.

After his return to France, Semprún published several books related to his experiences as an inmate in Buchenwald (*Le grand voyage* and *L'Évanouissement*); his experiences as an underground leader (*Autobiografía de Frederico Sanchez*); and his views on Stalinism (*La deuxieme mort de Ramón Mercader*). Completely trilingual in Spanish, French, and German, Semprún worked with distinguished directors on several important films dealing with crimes of fascism and Stalinism. Among the films were Alain Resnais's *La guerre est finie* and Costa-Gavras's *Z* and *L'Aveu*. *Z*, which won the Jury Prize at the 1969 Cannes Film Festival and the Oscar for Best Foreign Film in 1970, told the story of a political murder by the Greek military dictatorship; *L'Aveu* was internationally acclaimed as a critique of the Stalinist show trials. Between 1988 and 1993, Semprún served as the minister of culture for the post-Franco socialist government.

As a disgruntled former communist, Semprún was sensitive to the crimes committed by the Soviet Union in the gulag system. Both Alexandr Solzhenitsyn's *Gulag Archipelago* and Varlam Shalamov's *Kolyma Tales* are leitmotifs in Semprún's works. He grasped what totalitarianism meant in terms of European history and its legacy relating to Nazism and Stalinism.

Elie Wiesel and Jorge Semprún in Buchenwald

ELIE WIESEL, THE JEWISH "RACIAL" DEPORTEE, AND Jorge Semprún, the political inmate, were interned in Buchenwald at the same time, starting with Wiesel's arrival on January 26, 1945, and ending with their liberation on April 11 of the same year. Although they were in the same place, their experiences in the camp could not have been more different.

Tattooed with the number A-7713 in Auschwitz and registered as inmate 123565, Wiesel was assigned to block 57 in Buchenwald. Two days after his arrival, and sick himself, a powerless Wiesel witnessed the death of his father, Shlomo. Traumatized, the sixteen-year-old Wiesel, who arrived in Buchenwald exactly one year after Semprún, became numb to his surroundings, living in a haze of suffering and indifference.

Jorge Semprún had been registered as inmate 44904 and assigned to block 40 in Buchenwald. Upon his arrival, he was recognized as a fellow communist by the German anti-Nazi inmates in charge of administering those aspects of the camp's bureaucracy allocated to them by the SS. Semprún, who spoke flawless German, was given an assignment in the camp office that registered fellow inmates.

About Buchenwald

SITUATED FIVE MILES OUTSIDE WEIMAR, GERMANY, Buchenwald was built in 1937 by inmates under SS supervision. Its initial population consisted for the most part of German political inmates. The camp was originally to be called

KL Ettersberg after the nearby castle, but because of the association of this wooded region with German writer Johann Wolfgang von Goethe, Reichsführer-SS Heinrich Himmler decided on Buchenwald (beechwood). In the aftermath of Kristallnacht in November 1938, almost 10,000 Jews were transported to and interned in Buchenwald. Most were subsequently released on the condition that they leave Germany. Convicted criminals, Roma and Sinti, Jehovah's Witnesses, and German military deserters were also interned in Buchenwald. The transport of Jews after Kristallnacht increased the total number of prisoners in 1938 to 18,000; by the end of 1944, the total inmate population numbered 63,000. By February 1945, due to the forced evacuation of about 10,000 Jews from Auschwitz and Gross-Rosen and the arrival of other prisoners, the total number of inmates in Buchenwald rose to 86,000. On April 6, 1945, a few days before liberation, 28,500 Buchenwald prisoners were evacuated in a "death march." One in four inmates died during this march. From 1945 to 1950, Buchenwald was used by Soviet occupation forces as an NKVD (secret police) internment camp.

During World War II, the Buchenwald concentration camp was the center of an extensive network of subcamps and an important source of forced labor for the Reich. Initially, the administration of the camp was delegated to inmates interned as ordinary criminals, but starting in 1939, political prisoners, communists, Social Democrats, and others gradually replaced them. The underground communist network was especially active in the camp's Office of Labor Statistics, to which Semprún was assigned, and in the infirmary. Inmates working in the statistics office were able to protect other inmates from the SS by assigning them light work or even by assigning them the identities of prisoners who had died. Just before the liberation of the camp, the underground network sabotaged the SS's plans for another wave of evacuations, bringing an end to the death marches from Buchenwald. With firearms in hand, the inmates then attacked the remaining guards.

The communist underground network to which Jorge Semprún belonged saved Elie Wiesel's life. On the second page of a Buchenwald prisoner list dated February 9, 1945, prisoner 123565 (Wiesel) was categorized as "not able to be transported, held back for 4 weeks of light labor." On the second page of a list dated March 15, 1945, prisoner 123565 was identified by name as Wiesel L. (Lazar from Eliezer) and was given "two months of light labor."

Elie Wiesel and Jorge Semprún on the Holocaust and the Nazi Concentration Camp System

THIS VOLUME, A TRANSCRIPTION OF A DISCUSSION between Elie Wiesel and Jorge Semprún televised on the European cultural channel ARTE, has never before been published in English. The two men, famous in intellectual circles and well known to the Paris media, discuss the human condition under catastrophic circumstances. Semprún understands, as do very few others, the singularity of the destruction of European Jewry and its ties to both the industrial Nazi "Final Solution" and the centuries of antisemitic persecution. He states: "Entire communities were taken away.... It is a completely different experience. And what is so terrifying to me is that Europe has taken so long to admit, to recognize the uniqueness of this." Wiesel expresses the same thought: "What was fundamentally and profoundly unique was the plan, the enemy's project to annihilate an entire people to the last living being."[2]

In the course of the conversation, Semprún speaks of the categories of inmate in the Nazi concentration camp system: "The Nazi hierarchy ranked the camps according to whether a detainee could be reeducated or not. Of course, Jews were not to be 'reeducated.' They were to be exterminated." Wiesel agrees: "Buchenwald, that was a camp for political prisoners. So, in the beginning, they were supposed to reeducate the deportees, the prisoners. We Jews were there to die." Wiesel also emphasizes that the Nazi concentration system intended to destroy the identity of the inmates to the last degree: "I had my number, A7713. That was it. I was a number. And from time to time, someone from my village would simply remind me that I had a name."

The two former inmates of Buchenwald also agree on the tragic reason why the fate of the victims of Nazism was ignored for so long after the end of the war. "People turned away from those who were deported," says Semprún. Wiesel agrees: "People loved Resistance fighters, but they turned away from those who were deported. . . . Because we had indeed approached the abyss, the abyss of Humanity. We showed them what a human being is capable of doing. The good as well as the evil. These were the extreme limits. Nobody wanted to be confronted with this. We were an embarrassment; we made people uncomfortable."

Both Semprún and Wiesel struggle against the myths generated by the tragic history of the Holocaust and World War II. During his internment in Buchenwald, Semprún observed the arrival of a transport of Jews who were emaciated, terrified, and morally devastated, and this led him to reject the fallacy of Jewish passivity: "The myth of Jewish passivity is a foul myth. . . . Among the Jews there were many resistance fighters in all the European countries. I even believe that if one wrote the history of Jewish resistance, one would see how important a role it played; in France, at any rate, it's obvious." Wiesel cautions the public against the illusion of the end of evil with the defeat of Nazi Germany and its allies. "Evil survived Auschwitz. The victory of the Allies did not stop the existence of Evil. After fascism, there was still racial hatred, fanaticism that still exists in some ways almost everywhere." Wiesel also warned against the simplification of culpability: "Killing a child is the ultimate Evil. Killing one and a half million children—that is the ultimate Evil. . . . No, never will I believe that a young German is guilty simply because he is German. Only the guilty are guilty. The sons of the guilty, the children of the guilty are children. Guilt is limited, or unlimited if you like, to that category, to those who perpetrated the crime."

During a 2010 visit to Buchenwald, knowing that he would never return, Semprún paid tribute to the Jewish victims of the Holocaust:

> When all the witnesses, deported resistance fighters, have disappeared—soon, in a few years—there will yet remain one living memory, personal, of the concentration camp experience, a memory that will survive us, and that is the Jewish memory. The last man to remember, well after our death, will be one of those Jewish children we saw arriving in Buchenwald in February 1945, evacuated from Auschwitz, having miraculously survived the cold, the hunger, and the interminable voyage in freight cars, often open, to testify in the name of all the disappeared and the survivors, Jews and goys (non-Jews), the women and the men. Long life to the Jewish mourning of our death![3]

Where are we today, twenty-five years after this dialogue between Wiesel and Semprún took place, and after both have passed away?

We are living through a time that would certainly have outraged both men. A time during which humanism has been betrayed. A time during which ultranationalism and antisemitism are on the rise again. A time during which some European governments are rewriting the history of the Holocaust, insulting its victims.

We miss Elie Wiesel and Jorge Semprún, their smiles, and their wisdom. This book is a small homage to them.

GALLERY OF PHOTOGRAPHS

Mass arrest of Jews following Kristallnacht, labeled "the Jewish action," November 1938.

Arrival of Polish prisoners. Date unknown (post-1937).

Arrival of Polish prisoners. Date unknown (post-1937).

Arrival of Dachau concentration camp inmates to Buchenwald.
Date unknown (post-1937).

Dachau concentration camp inmates after their arrival in Buchenwald. Date unknown (post-1937).

Dachau concentration camp inmates during a roll call after their arrival in Buchenwald. Date unknown (post-1937).

Arrival of Czech prisoners. Date unknown (post-1937).

Arrival of Czech prisoners. Date unknown (post-1937).

A roll call during the construction of the Buchenwald camp. Date unknown (1937?).

A roll call in the Buchenwald camp. Date unknown (post-1937).

Heinrich Himmler during an inspection of Buchenwald. Date unknown (post-1937).

IT IS IMPOSSIBLE TO REMAIN SILENT

Jorge Semprún At a certain point in your *Memoirs*, when you evoke the shock of your arrival in Buchenwald after the evacuation of Auschwitz, you say—citing me, and in reference to conversations that we had later on, much later on—that our experiences in the camp were not at all the same. Which is absolutely true. Perhaps, to get us started, we can emphasize this diversity—not just the diversity of our personal experiences in this particular camp, which was Buchenwald, in January, February, and March 1945, but also the more global, more general diversity among the different camps. In the archipelago of the Nazi concentration camp system, there were many differences. I would like to start our conversation here, from this diversity of experience.

Elie Wiesel All right, first there is Auschwitz. Death camp. Camp full of the dead. And Buchenwald, as you well know, was something quite different—more politicized, more political in nature—in the beginning. Therefore, for us, Buchenwald was supposed to be a different type of camp. But for us, the Little Camp,[1] inside the main camp, was almost like Auschwitz, except there was no gas chamber. Of course, in the complex of concentration camps, some camps were a little better than others, different from others. We knew all the names; I remember that, even at Auschwitz, I heard the names of Sachsenhausen, Ravensbrück, Bergen-Belsen. We knew a little bit about that universe. But Buchenwald, seen from Auschwitz, was supposed to be a better camp. But that was not the case.

J. S. In the Nazi system, there were bureaucratic specificities for each camp. It is really incredible to read these documents. The classifications they themselves created. The Nazi hierarchy ranked the camps according to whether a detainee could be reeducated or not. Of course, Jews were not to be "reeducated." They were to be exterminated. So already there was that category.

E. W. Nonetheless, there were indeed people who were to be reeducated at Auschwitz—the homosexuals. But Buchenwald, that was a camp for political prisoners. So, in the beginning, they were supposed to reeducate the deportees, the prisoners. We Jews were there to die.

J. S. Absolutely.

E. W. Just as they were there to kill us, we were there to die. And Buchenwald, our camp, was made for this. Every time we have gotten together, over the years, I have wondered what it was that you saw, what it was that I saw there. And of course, it was not the same thing.

J. S. Because in Buchenwald there were two camps, the main camp and the quarantine camp or Little Camp, which remained in place until just about the autumn of 1944, when the Germans had practically lost the war. At that point, conditions deteriorated in all the camps—even in the forced labor camps, not just the extermination camps. This Little Camp was a transit camp, a quarantine camp; people went through it to be integrated into the Buchenwald system to produce weapons of war—factories, et cetera—or they were sent to other *Kommandos*, other camps. From that time on, the Little Camp became a permanent camp. People remained there.

E. W. People remained there.

J. S. They were there to die.

E. W. To die.

J. S. And so, from then on, in fact, and especially after the arrival of the surviving Jews from Auschwitz—if you take away the gas chamber—the living conditions, the conditions of brutality and lack of hygiene, the overcrowding resembled certain camps in the Auschwitz-Birkenau complex. And for us [the political prisoners], that was a decisive moment, because when you arrived, and those from other camps in [occupied] Poland arrived, we had—we had had a vague notion that the camps in Poland were worse—but all of a sudden, we had concrete proof. Listening to your stories, and through the discussions we had with some of you, we saw what it was. And we saw that another, deeper circle existed, worse than Hell.

E. W. We did have our own circle. In fact, for us it started a little bit earlier. It started in August for Buchenwald. We were evacuated on the eighteenth [of January 1945]. On the nineteenth, we were herded into a train, meaning open freight cars; it was snowing. It took us several days. That particular trip, I cannot forget. I remember, just before we arrived, it was afternoon in Weimar. We had no idea where we were. It was snowing. Already there were deaths. Many dead in the open cars. I was with my father. And all of a sudden, we went mad. Each one of us had three blankets, and we had lost all hope. We went mad. And we started to shout out a prayer—the prayer that is usually read at the end of Yom Kippur, the Day of Atonement, "The Lord is God." When I think about it now, I still can't believe it. It was a sort of farewell to life, a farewell to the world. And we were going to die. Everyone knew it. We were going to die. Each one of us knew it. Each one had convinced himself. So then, we all started swaying back and forth together, as we had at the synagogue when I was a kid "The Lord is God." We had all gone mad. Then the train stopped at Weimar. And all of a sudden, we heard several deportees tell us that Buchenwald had refused to bring us in. Because the camp was already overcrowded. We did not pay any attention. The Lord is God. We shouted, "The Lord is God." They did bring us in. I remember night had already fallen. At long last, a shower. You describe that in your book; I describe it in mine. And then, there we were in the Little Camp. And in the beginning, the Little Camp was almost worse for me, worse than Auschwitz.

J. S. During the fall of 1944, I had gotten into the habit of going into the Little Camp to visit certain friends, certain people who were, for example, in barrack 56—the infirmary. [Maurice] Halbwachs, who was my professor at the Sorbonne, and [Henri] Maspero, the father of François Maspero, who was a well-respected specialist in Oriental studies.[2] And we saw what the conditions were like in the Little Camp. But all of a sudden, conditions deteriorated radically.

E. W. Late January. I remember that, to keep us away from the large quarantine barrack, they sprayed us with water. With freezing water in front of the barrack. We turned into blocks of ice. And I was with my father. But then again, the father I knew was no longer there. That father was dead. And then, in fact, I was no longer conscious of Buchenwald. I was no longer alive. From that day on until the Liberation, I was simply no longer there.

J. S. Yes, you talk about that in your book. All those weeks, where mechanically, almost without being conscious of what you were doing, you accomplished a number of tasks, and sometimes you even played chess without realizing what you were doing at the same time. You were already . . .

E. W. I was no longer there. I had stayed alive only for my father. Because I knew that my little sister, my mother, were no longer there. Of course I hoped that my older sisters were still alive. But this was my father. You see, you had an active life inside the main camp, you knew why you were there, you were a resister, you were fighting for a cause, you were part of the [French] Resistance. I was a *Musulman,* as they used to say at that time; I was just an object.[3] I had no idea what was going on around me.

J. S. That is the other great difference, that continues throughout History, and that we have to come back to because it is essential to our understanding. The terrifying singularity of the Nazi system was, and shall forever be, in the memory of the survivors and in actual History for future generations— that cold decision, put into action in a systematic, industrial, rational way, to exterminate an entire people.

E. W. To the last one.

J. S. To the last one.

E. W. Literally, to the last one.

J. S. It is merely by chance that this was not the "Final Solution," but it gradually came close to becoming the Final Solution. So the implementation of a systematic industry of destruction—the gas chambers and all that went with them— makes the experience totally different, and then there is the difference of actually living through that experience. Because yes, it's true, the resistance fighters took a certain number of risks; they knew full well that they risked being arrested and then tortured, deported, or put before a firing squad. And it was a solitary experience and, at the same time, one of great solidarity, because we were alone but in groups, networks, political parties. You went through a family experience. Entire families were taken away . . .

E. W. Entire communities.

J. S. Entire communities were taken away. The destruction—you know it, you see the destruction, you see it progressively, you identify it. It has the face of a mother, a sister, a cousin, a friend from a village in Romania, in Hungary, or in

Poland. It is a completely different experience. And what is so terrifying to me is that Europe has taken so long to admit, to recognize the uniqueness of this.

E. W. Not yet. Not yet. Not all of Europe.

J. S. Not all Europe, not all Europeans. Still, we have made progress, due in part to your own reaction to what you lived through. Breaking the silence, the silence of horror that there was among the Jewish survivors of the genocide. You remained silent upon your return, because no one paid any attention, because you were not among the heroes of this History. And that—that is terrifying.

E. W. No one wanted to listen to us. Because we were considered shameful to Humanity. People pitied us. Personally, it took me ten years to start to talk about it, and to be honest, I do not talk about it much; I do not speak well. Yes, that's true. But you have to admit—no one wanted to listen to us.

J. S. Moreover, experience shows us that the first books, the first great books that were written—I am referring to the narratives of those in the Resistance . . .

E. W. People loved resistance fighters, but they turned away from those who were deported.

J. S. People turned away from those who were deported.

E. W. Because we had indeed approached the abyss, the abyss of Humanity. We showed them what a human being is capable of doing. The Good as well as the Evil. These were the extreme limits. Nobody wanted to be confronted with this. We were an embarrassment; we made people uncomfortable.

J. S. We made them uncomfortable. We made them uncomfortable. It was a time of endings, of the end of the war. It was a time when people idealized the circumstances. We had defeated fascism; we somehow felt that, in certain respects, it was the end of a terrible part of twentieth-century history and the beginning of something new. And we blocked it out of our minds, erased it. We also erased from our consciousness for a long time, because it was something that was associated with the winning side, the experience in Russian camps. We blocked that out, too. No one wanted to hear about that, either. Even we deportees did not want to listen. I am speaking about myself. I couldn't bear to hear about that particular experience, because it seemed impossible to believe. Even more unbelievable than the other one [in the Nazi camps]. It has been a long process. I am under the impression that, today, fifty years later, after all . . .

E. W. It is the young who make the difference. The young people today want to know. To be frank, what I like best is to speak to the young. To have young people ask me questions, in America and here. Young people listen. Because they say that it is their last chance to hear a witness. You or I, we are witnesses. And so they come. They listen with real interest. They listen with healthy curiosity, with their soul, with their vision. They listen with their entire being, because they realize that it is an experience they will never know.

J. S. Because they know that they will never experience that, because there is a distance. The same thing happens to me. It has always been difficult, or unpleasant, or I have considered it useless to speak about this experience to people of my generation, et cetera. Whereas now, I do not say that it has become easy, but at least, it has become possible.

E. W. Possible . . . No, Jorge, it is impossible, but we do it anyway. We have no choice.

J. S. Impossible from a metaphysical point of view. If you like. Of course. Impossible. But nonetheless possible because they are not implicated or guilty. It isn't their story. That is why they have a viewpoint about this part of History that is, at one and the same time, direct, more open—you might even say, more insolent. They are able to ask questions.

E. W. And so generous. Generous. They are generous in that they want to listen and are receptive to our experiences, which shows their generosity. That touches me deeply.

J. S. That is something I've experienced, I think, even when it comes to the family—I do not know what your experience is, you are going to tell me—but even when it comes to the family, we have found that it is easier to talk to our grandchildren than to our children.

E. W. Indeed, absolutely. We skip a generation.

J. S. As if a certain amount of time had to pass for things to mature. Objectively, historically, all that time had to pass before people started reading books.

E. W. People did not read them. People did not read them because, to tell you the truth—that is, if you like, the hopeless part of this story—this story will never be known. What you and I saw, no one will ever see. We try. Really, we do everything in our power. I do not think they see.

J. S. We write sometimes—we do not write all the time; we do not write only about that, neither you nor I do—we write knowing that there are things that cannot . . .

E. W. . . . that cannot be said.

J. S. We cannot say everything, incite the imagination to see every single thing, make people understand everything. Obviously, that cannot be done.

E. W. To keep silent is forbidden, yet to speak is impossible. I have always been afraid of losing my memory. I know that memory is vulnerable. It crumbles into pieces. Are there things I have forgotten? Are there faces that I no longer recognize, that are no longer in my mind's eye? Are there everyday actions that have vanished, things I can no longer accomplish? So what can I do? How can I go about telling everything, telling what has to be told? The writer that I am, and that you are, cannot avoid asking these very questions.

J. S. What I am talking about is my relationship to writing as a writer. I had to remain silent during a certain period of time—fifteen years—in order to survive. As a matter of fact, it seems to be an experience many shared. Others came back to life by writing. Primo Levi. Others came back to life because they succeeded in writing something quickly. Came back to life, temporarily.

E. W. Primo Levi committed suicide, I believe, I am convinced, because he was a writer. He was a friend of mine. I met him after the war.

J. S. Because the relationship to writing is complex . . .

E. W. There are quite a few authors who committed suicide.

J. S. [Jean] Améry, Levi, and others, of course.

E. W. Or Paul Celan.

J. S. But then, strangely enough, something rather odd happens regarding my relationship to memory, regarding my fear of forgetting. The more I write—three of my books are directly related to my experience in the camps, even if, in the other books, the references are much more indirect, novelistic, so to speak, [because] it is the characters, it is not I who have this type of relationship—the more I write, the more memories come flooding in. That is to say, after this last book, I have even more to say than before I started the first one. It is as if the loss of memory was so profound that it was necessary to undertake the task of writing, voluntary memory, voluntary research into the past, so that the images, the memories, the faces, anecdotes, even sensations could come back to me. That's the basis of my theory—that this type of writing is inexhaustible, at one and the same time impossible and inexhaustible. It is impossible to recount what happened, but we will never have said everything. Each time, we can say more.

E. W. Recently, I dreamed that I was writing. I dream more and more often about that period of my life. In the beginning, during the war, we dreamed about other things, about food, about peace. When I was living at home, I dreamed about Shabbat, Jewish holidays, my family. Then, after liberation, it was different. And now, more and more often, almost every night, it's a sort of nightmare. I find myself there again. In the morning, I get up, and very quickly I jot down what I remember from those dreams. Because, to tell the truth, not all will be told.

J. S. Writing also revives memory, and it can't help but revive anguish. The therapy of amnesia played a soothing role during a certain period of my life. Involvement in politics played another role, because it gives one the illusion that there's a future—at any rate, communist politics does. Then the failure of this illusion brings one back to writing, to one's own memory. And the more I write, the more insistent memory becomes, but naturally, the anguish comes back, too.

E. W. It all comes down to this for me: We discovered absolute Evil. And not absolute Good. So what can we do for the young people who are kind enough to read what we have written or to listen to us, so that they won't fall into despair? How can we go about telling them that it is nonetheless given to man to thirst for the absolute in Good and not only in Evil?

J. S. Absolute Evil can be found. The Good is hard to find. Good, or the path towards the Good.

E. W. That is absolutely true. I myself remember, and that is the victory of memory. I had forgotten everything, even my name. At the end of my time in Auschwitz, and above all, on the train. I had my number, A7713. That was it. I was a number. And from time to time, someone from my village would simply remind me that I had a name. Someone called me by my name. At first it was my father, of course. And in the Little Camp in Buchenwald, I had a friend, a little boy from Kovno in

Lithuania, who called me by my name. And that was enough for me, to be able to believe that man was capable of Good.

J. S. As a matter of fact, I have a question for you. I'll answer it, too. Let's both try to answer it. What meaning can we give to this series of commemorations, of recollections, of publications, of testimonies, related to the fiftieth anniversary of the liberation of the camps, of the victory over Nazism—a victory that is not a total victory over the totalitarian system because it has continued in the Soviet Union for a long time? There are commemorations, people ask us things. What should we do?

E. W. I go to this sort of commemoration with a heavy heart. And against my will. I do not like it. To tell you the truth, I really do not like it. But there is no choice, no alternative. I would prefer to go to the site alone, or with someone who was with me at the time. To be there alone, two or three of us, but be there alone and not say anything. And to try to cry, if possible. Or to stop crying, if that were possible. But I do not like all of that. At the same time, I remind myself that those who did not live through this need something symbolic—some sites where they can focus their desire to know what happened, their thirst to know. It is for them that we attend this type of ceremony, be it for Buchenwald or for Auschwitz. Deep inside, it disturbs me. I don't know. I am supposed to speak, and I always feel like saying something else. And I have sometimes stopped right in the middle of a sentence, because I could tell I was going to cry. I do not like crying in public. Even when I am alone, I do not like to cry.

J. S. But that is a feeling we can't avoid when we're on stage, so to speak, with other witnesses talking about that. There is always a moment when we ask ourselves, "What am I doing here? Why did I come?" It's inevitable. We cannot avoid it. We regain our composure. We distance ourselves. We delve deep into our own memories. We get over it nonetheless in order to accomplish this pedagogical rite of bearing witness.

We are elsewhere. And sometimes, we are very far away. And so far away that we wish ... We wish we could disappear....

E. W. And we do disappear. . . . Inside ourselves, we disappear.

J. S. I believe that it is completely normal and inevitable. However, I wonder whether, in order to address young people and their curiosity, their need to know, we shouldn't try, instead of going back in time fifty years, we shouldn't start with the present. That is to say, take examples from what is going on today, not confuse ...

E. W. Nor compare. One should never compare.

J. S. Nor compare. We must not fall into the trap of May '68, where they used the slogan "CRS-SS," which is absurd.[4]

E. W. Or else talk about Auschwitz in Serbia today.

J. S. Or talk of Auschwitz in Serbia. But still, just one example: Ethnic cleansing permits [us], without making a comparison or an amalgam, or trying to say that Auschwitz is already there, because that is ... it's simply monstrous to say that, to try to comprehend the totalitarian mechanisms that were at work and which rear their heads again in various places, from time to time. I wonder if it would not be better to go further back—I don't know, it's a question I ask myself—so that the lesson could be more effective. So that commemorations are not simply a ritual of remembrance but a concrete act—political, in the larger sense of the term—for the young people of today.

E. W. You understand these things—you were active in politics, you were a government minister, so you know something about politics—but I don't, not at all. I am a teacher. I am a storyteller. I teach humanities and social studies, so I have students. There are students who take off from the present heading towards the past and students who prefer to start with the past; and then, we all come back, do we not, to the present.

J. S. The essential thing is that there is a path. That is to say, a connection involving an experience or a current event, a connection to an experience that permits one precisely—I am coming back to my point—to emphasize the diversity, the exceptional uniqueness of the extermination of the Jewish people, which differentiates it from all other experiences involving concentration camps. Because more people may have died in the *gulag* of Kolyma than died at Auschwitz. But it is not the same thing.

E. W. It is not the same thing. But, Jorge, Evil survived Auschwitz. The victory of the Allies did not stop the existence of Evil. After fascism, there was still racial hatred, fanaticism that still exists in some ways almost everywhere. But one must never compare situations. Of course, we still live inside a century, the same century, the most violent century in History. I believe that during that time, History released, revealed, and liberated so many dark and malevolent forces that even today we are reeling from the effects. And we sense these effects exactly in ethnic cleansing, as you say, or in Rwanda—actually, all over the world. The planet has become a small family, a small village, but agitated by terrible and terrifying currents. And we feel them. So, we remember—of course we remember, we cannot help but remember. When I see a little girl or a little boy on television, dying in the arms of a mother somewhere in Africa or Chechnya, it hurts. It hurts. When I hear, you know, that they are killing intellectuals in Algeria, it reminds me of Germany in 1933, not the Holocaust, but 1933. It hurts. It hurts all the more because I am under the impression that I am watching something grow. It's growing. And if Auschwitz and Buchenwald did not really change man, then what will change him?

J. S. We cannot define man. Evil as inhuman.

E. W. Everything is human.

J. S. Yes. We are getting down to the core, that which is central to the camp experience. That is to say, the discovery that human freedom, the freedom of man is a freedom capable of both Good and Evil. Of Good, because we have known waves of solidarity, of extraordinary self-sacrifice.

E. W. Outside [the camps] too. All those who risked their lives to save Jews, for example. These are heroes, resistance fighters. Of course.

J. S. I think that we have to persevere in this direction. Because if we commemorate something that occurred, as if it were some horrible thing that took place in the past—"fifty years ago, it was like this"—and we forget first and foremost that the liberators of Auschwitz—those who really liberated Auschwitz, and not only Auschwitz, but who also won the battle of Stalingrad and pushed forward all the way to Berlin— came from a country where there were camps, too. Where camps still existed even ten, fifteen years later. That there were replications of this even later than that. In Yugoslavia, those who talk about ethnic cleansing are not rooted—even if it ends up being that—in Nazi ideology, but in communism. So it is true, we cannot just commemorate something and stop there, we must . . .

E. W. We must place everything into the context of the present, in reality. But you know, you talk about the liberation of the camps, but I asked General [Vasilii] Petrenko a question about that years ago, in Moscow. It was he who liberated Auschwitz. We were there. We compared our impressions of our last night there. Those of us inside the camp, we were getting ready to come out, and he was preparing his troops to liberate the camp. I asked him the question, "Two days earlier, you could have ordered your troops to surge forward; you would have saved the lives of one hundred thousand men and women. And you did not do it. Why? Why not?" And he started to explain this and that. . . . It's not that simple. It's the same for the Allied troops. They could have liberated Buchenwald earlier. They came upon Buchenwald by accident. It was not a priority.

J. S. It was not a strategic priority. But the Allies could have, those in the West could have, especially from 1943 on, made known to the public what they knew about the extermination that was underway, threatened the enemy directly . . .

E. W. And bombed the railroad tracks to Auschwitz. And the Russians could have, too, for that matter. They were even closer.

J. S. Actually, they could have intervened. Revealed the list of names they already had—because the Jewish Resistance had already turned it over to them. Made dozens and dozens of Germans accountable for their actions. "This is what the Nazis are. This is what is going to happen to you." Announce Nuremberg in this way. No one did. No one did for the same reasons that people continued to keep silent afterwards.

E. W. I visited Babi Yar. In 1965, there was nothing there. Later, they put up a monument, but at Babi Yar, sixty thousand to eighty thousand Jews were killed in ten days, between Rosh Hashanah and Yom Kippur. Not a single reference to the Jews. There wasn't a single Jew there, among the communists, among the Russians. It was the same for Auschwitz.

J. S. It was the same for Auschwitz. It was a camp where the antifascists died. All of a sudden, they erase, they obliterate the profound truth about Auschwitz—that it was the extermination camp for the Final Solution.

E. W. They killed the Jews a second time.

J. S. They killed the Jews a second time. In regards to Babi Yar, we had to wait for the poem by [Yevgeny] Yevtushenko and a gradual thaw [in East-West relations].

E. W. And even then!

J. S. It was contested; it was precarious and fragile.

E. W. They finally put up a monument, only recently. Two years ago, they put up a Jewish monument. But on the main monument, not a word about the Jews. "Here died Soviet citizens." As if the Jews of Kiev were gunned down because they were Soviet citizens or communists. When you think about it . . . all that could have been done to stop them before, even during the war, in fact. So many people could have been saved. I cannot seem to get rid of a taste, a profound sense of melancholy. That said, we carry on, and we keep on trying. Soon, we will no longer be around. We have to leave a trace.

J. S. In Buchenwald we used to get together on Sunday afternoons and form discussion groups. And in one of the groups where there weren't any Jews—because there were very few Jews surviving in the main camp—we got together to talk about, to discuss the existence of God. This wasn't a problem for you?

E. W. Yes, this was a problem. But for me, God was still my anchor. I do not understand, Jorge, I cannot conceive of Auschwitz and Buchenwald with God or without God. And every time, I keep asking myself the question, "But God in all this, what was He doing, where was He?" You see, I come from a deeply religious milieu. Very religious. You, you come from a milieu of political activists. After all, you were a Resistance fighter. You worked at it. I did nothing. I just let things happen. It was God who made things, and man destroyed them—events, living beings. So for me, God was everything, because man, at any rate, was worthless in my eyes. It was God who counted. It was He who gave my life meaning. It was He who was the justification for all that was happening to me. And here, I sensed that there was a void, an eclipse. But where was God? So I fought Him, later, especially after the war. When I started studying philosophy, when I learned how to formulate questions. But God was always there. Even in the Little Camp, I remember, it was Passover. During Passover we are not allowed to eat bread. All right, I ate it anyway. But I had friends who did not eat it, even inside the camp. I remember prayers. Prayers were said the day of Passover in the Little Camp. And me, I was just there, but not really there. The first thing we did on the eleventh of April, a small group of friends in the camp, was to recite the Kaddish.[5] The Kaddish for the dead. That was the very first thing we did; that was it—recite the Kaddish. So I defined myself through my relationship to God. And up to this very day, I still don't know.

J. S. That is the main difference in your testimony; in other testimonies by religious Jews about the camps, we can sense very intensely that this attachment, this religion, this connection, this attachment to God is part of how you resisted. Despite all the absurdity, the incomprehensibility, the total madness of the destiny of the Jewish people, there is this attachment. Of course, there are also other attachments possible, because among the Jews there were many resistance fighters in all the European countries. I even believe that if one wrote the history of Jewish resistance, one would see how important a role it played; in France, at any rate, it's obvious—in the combat groups, in the "shock" groups . . .[6]

E. W. . . . in Birkenau in the *Kommando* [slave labor detachment] centers, in the Warsaw Ghetto. Sobibór.

J. S. The myth of Jewish passivity is a foul myth. All right. But there is this attachment to moral resistance, a moral identity that is very strong, that is a totally different construct for us. I come from a Catholic family; it's true that I have been an atheist since adolescence, and yet it was those group discussions we had in Buchenwald that ultimately led me to define my relationship with God. Ultimately they led me to believe that the debate about distances is ungrounded, because as long as there are men there will be God. There will always be this relationship with something that transcends us. So it is not the question of existence that should be discussed; there are other questions. That is something I learned [from], or is the consequence of, those Sunday discussion groups in Buchenwald. That is to say, you have to push atheism, if I dare say paradoxically, to its very limits. And when you push atheism to its very limits, you realize that it is a need that is thoroughly human, a totally human desire, a fantasy that is human, a human necessity. It will always be there, as long as there are men.

E. W. As far as I am concerned, there were two pivotal moments—without including my father's death. The first moment of terror was our arrival in Birkenau. It was night-time. There were thousands—it seemed to me that there were thousands of Jews coming from all directions and heading toward the flames. And I, I was terrified; I said to myself, this is the end of the Jewish people. The second moment was much later, when I asked myself the question that the Sages had already been asking themselves a long time ago. There comes a time when you have to ask yourself, "Has God had enough of his chosen people? Has he changed sides?" And when I said to myself, "And God in all this?" I was really asking myself the question, "And what if God no longer were on my side, but on the enemy's side?" And then I came to the conclusion "Perhaps God can become the enemy, but the enemy is not God."

J. S. That, too, is something I perceived very strongly in the Jewish experience in the camps. There were Catholics who were deported, there were Protestants deported. God certainly played a role in their daily existence, in their solitude. No religious services were permitted in the concentration camps, no religious practice of any kind. But I would say that for the other deportees, this is secondary in their testimonies; it is not of the first order of importance. It was a private affair. God is a private affair, whereas what the Jewish people experienced—their deportation, their extermination—is something else. That, too, is a unique experience. It is something else.

E. W. What was fundamentally and profoundly unique was the plan, the enemy's project to annihilate an entire people to the last living being. Children yet to be born were already condemned to death. When I think about the children . . . the children bring tears to my eyes. When I think about the children—beautiful, discreet, tender, we see their photos now, don't we?—who went calmly, quietly, without crying, without complaining, to their death. I ask myself, How could they do it? You know, Jorge, I hope that the killers will never be pardoned. I do not want God to pardon them for what they did to the children. Never.

J. S. Yes. Of course. The children in the camps were Jewish children.

E. W. Those are the ones who bear the responsibility for this crime. Because killing a child is the ultimate Evil. Killing one and a half million children—that is the ultimate Evil. No pardon should ever be granted to those who were responsible for those crimes. That said, I'll give you an example: In Germany, I have students. In my classes, I have young students who are German. I don't teach this. I teach philosophy, literature. I do not teach about the Holocaust. It's the Germans who come to speak to me, and some of them feel guilty. And I say to them, you absolutely must not feel that way. You are not guilty. You are not guilty for what your grandparents or your parents did. I do not believe in collective guilt. I never believed in it. As a Jew, I know that my people have suffered greatly precisely because we have been accused of so many things, and we were forced to bear this collective guilt. No, never will I believe that a young German is guilty simply because he is German. Only the guilty are guilty. The sons of the guilty, the children of the guilty are children. Guilt is limited, or unlimited if you like, to that category, to those who perpetrated the crime.

J. S. I would even go so far as to say that a great majority of German youth have come to terms with the past and the relationship that their country and their people have with memory, something that younger generations from other countries have yet to do.

E. W. Nonetheless they feel more implicated than others.

J. S. . . . still very sensitive. You can see how they react to certain statements made by politicians or certain statements by journalists or certain actions by violent neo-Nazi groups or those who commit acts of profanation at racist demonstrations. The reaction of youth—in the larger sense of the term, not just adolescents, but of the new Germany—is immediate. These things lead me to believe that hope is possible.

E. W. I am very hopeful that, thanks to these young people, hope has a future.

J. S. The future promises to be all the more hopeful because, for all sorts of historical, social, and economic reasons, Germany's role in Europe is decisive. The new Germany, and those Germans who will hold leadership positions in the year 2000, will, in this way, be profoundly anchored in the memory of fundamental democratic values, which are values of tolerance, a denial to forgetfulness, a refusal to forget. I believe that this is important.

E. W. All the same. How could the killers have killed? How could the world stand by and do nothing? That, I do not know. Ultimately we are left with the same questions. I still have questions. And I do not have answers. We have to remember with gratitude what the underground resistance did in the camp. I owe them my life. Because the *Lagerschütz*, the camp police force, was made up of members of the resistance and run by them. And on April 5, when they evacuated all the Jews, it was those people, the camp policemen themselves, who told us, "Go back [to your barracks], go back!"

J. S. That is one of the unique things about Buchenwald. Due to the great number of German political prisoners, it was possible to organize international resistance groups, which included the communists and also the members of the French Committee. All the resistance networks were represented by the French Committee. When the SS issued the order to evacuate, communication between the *Lagerälteste*[7] and the SS had been severed. There was a sort of double life [inside the camp]. We were surrounded. The submachine guns were poised. This sort of double life resulted in the order to resist evacuation, to stay put as long as possible. From then on, the *Lagerschütz*, the camp police, prisoners, and other leaders tried to hold you back and told you "Don't go out to the *Appelplatz*;[8] let's try to hold out . . ."

E. W. Rather than our going out to roll call, they sent us back.

J. S. They sent us back to the blocks to try to prevent a bloodbath. And ultimately, that is how the lives of more than half of the prisoners were saved. Only when a German commando overran the camp were they able to force some of the prisoners to go out and line up, but only a small number.

E. W. It was April 11, and we were supposed to leave. You were, too. The camp was supposed to be liquidated.

J. S. The camp was to be liquidated. And then, they did not succeed in wiping it out. On April 11, the Americans had pushed past the camp and tanks surrounded it. There was an order . . .

E. W. . . . the uprising.

J. S. The uprising. And then all of a sudden, weapons that had been hidden for years appeared. Of course, we mustn't succumb to mythology. We cannot deny that the US Army liberated Buchenwald. But the actual participation of a few hundred armed men was of symbolic value, of moral and political value, in some ways. The Americans discovered a camp that was partially liberated, partially occupied . . .

E. W. . . . liberated, almost. To tell you the truth, I didn't even know that there was a resistance network inside Buchenwald. I was so far removed from all that after my father died that I did not know what was real, what was alive or not. I didn't even know that a resistance network at Buchenwald existed. I don't know how it was for you, but I remember that in the Little Camp, where we were, there was no celebration, no joy. The camp was liberated. And we just stood there. We looked at each other. We prayed. We recited the Kaddish. We were still in the grip of the past.

J. S. What joy? You already were far beyond feeling that.

E. W. Precisely, we were beyond that.

J. S. You were beyond that; you were already among the dead.

E. W. We were incapable of experiencing joy. We were still in the grip of death.

J. S. You were still in the grip of death.

E. W. There was no joy.

J. S. Even in the main camp, some of the prisoners did not feel any joy. Until a few days later, they may not even have entirely grasped what had occurred. We were still in the grip of death. Only a small minority could, not exactly feel joy as such, but experience a rather strange emotion. Our wildest dream had become reality. Statistics teach us that there are always some survivors who will live to tell the story of what happened. But we thought that it would be someone else.

E. W. How many stories were not told because there were no survivors.

J. S. How many stories are still not told today because certain survivors do not speak? Because we are a minority who do speak. Whatever efforts are deployed, whatever the difficulties, we are a small minority who actually speak. The majority of survivors do not speak.

E. W. Nonetheless, more and more do so. I think that now they sense that it's the end of the century. More and more. I receive manuscripts by the dozens, asking for a preface or a recommendation. They are speaking more. It was for them that I wrote my first book. To tell them that they must speak. However inadequate the means, we have to speak. We do not have the means, we don't possess the proper vocabulary, but we must speak. We must bear witness. And now they are starting to do so, more and more. I sense it.

J. S. Because it is the end. Because we are approaching the moment when there will be no more survivors. So, faced with a realization that the end is imminent, faced with this incomprehension on one side and on the other, faced with the comprehension of a new generation, people are opening up. This is true. As a matter of fact, I've been struck these past weeks that in the press, newspapers, magazines . . . I've been struck to see just how many new testimonies there are. People who hadn't said anything until now.

E. W. Who haven't said anything yet.

J. S. Who, forty-seven years later, fifty years later, agree to talk about certain things, say certain things. I find that very . . .

E. W. . . . reassuring. I imagine that one day, perhaps some years hence, we shall find the last survivor.

J. S. That is an obsession . . .

E. W. It's my personal obsession. I would not like to be in his place.

J. S. I think about that man or that woman, if he in fact finds this out, because he won't know. Just imagine a TV crew arrives and says to the person "Monsieur, or Madame, you are the very last survivor." What does he do? He commits suicide.

E. W. No. I would like to think that they would ask questions; they would ask him every question under the sun. And I mean every single one. And he will listen to all the questions. And afterwards, he'll shrug his shoulders. And they will say "So . . . ?" And he will say . . .

J. S. If he doesn't commit suicide, then he'll remain silent. It comes down to one and the same thing.

E. W. It's a pregnant silence. The very last. I would not like to be the very last survivor.

J. S. Nor would I.

March 1, 1995

NOTES

Introduction

1. Translated from the French by Marion Wiesel, with a new preface by the author; foreword by François Mauriac (New York: Hill and Wang, 2006), 34.

2. All quotes here and in the next three paragraphs are from the interview "It Is Impossible to Remain Silent," as translated in this volume.

3. Jorge Semprún, "Mon dernier voyage à Buchenwald," *Le Monde*, March 6, 2010.

It Is Impossible to Remain Silent

1. Kleines Lager.

2. François Maspero later became an editor of controversial books on censored subjects, such as the use of torture during the hostilities in Algeria. A committed leftist, he owned a bookstore in the Latin Quarter. The shop became a gathering place for political activists.

3. *Musulman* was a slang term used in Nazi concentration camps for emaciated and exhausted inmates who appeared resigned to their impending death.

4. During the student-worker uprising of May 1968 in France, which paralyzed the country and challenged the establishment and Charles de Gaulle's presidency, demonstrators tore up paving stones, set up barricades, occupied factories and universities, took over theaters and the Cannes Film Festival, and more. The *Compagnies républicaines de sécurité* (CRS) are a section of the police force trained to intervene during demonstrations and restore the peace. The group was created by de Gaulle in 1944. During the

uprising in 1968, the demonstrators taunted the CRS with slogans implying that they were as cruel as the Nazi SS.

5. Buchenwald was liberated on that day.

6. Units of the Resistance engaged in sabotage, for example placing explosives, making armed attacks, and carrying out targeted assassinations.

7. The most senior prisoner functionaries in the camp.

8. The campgrounds used for roll call.

SELECTED BIBLIOGRAPHIES OF JORGE SEMPRÚN AND ELIE WIESEL

SELECTED BIBLIOGRAPHY OF JORGE SEMPRÚN

Books

Le Grand Voyage. Paris: Gallimard, 1963.
L'Évanouissement. Paris: Gallimard, 1967.
La Deuxième Mort de Ramón Mercader. Paris: Gallimard, 1969.
Montand, la vie continue. Paris: Denoël, 1983.
La Montagne blanche. Paris: Gallimard, 1986.
Federico Sánchez vous salue bien. Paris: Grasset, 1993.
L'écriture ou la vie. Paris: Gallimard, 1994.
Le mort qu'il faut. Paris: Gallimard, 2001.
Quel beau dimanche! [1980]. Paris: Grasset, 2002.

Films

La Guerre est finie, 1966 / Alain Resnais, director; Jorge Semprún,
     screenwriter.
Z, 1969 / Costa-Gavras, director; Jorge Semprún, dialogues.
L'aveu, 1970 / Costa-Gavras, director; Jorge Semprún, screenwriter.
Stavisky, 1974 / Alain Resnais, director; Jorge Semprún,
     screenwriter.
Une Femme à sa fenêtre, 1976 / Pierre Granier-Deferre, director;
     Jorge Semprún, dialogues.
Les Routes du sud, 1978 / Joseph Losey, director; Jorge Semprún,
     screenwriter.
L'Affaire Dreyfus, 1995 / Yves Boisset, director, dialogues; Jorge
     Semprún, screenwriter, dialogues.

SELECTED BIBLIOGRAPHY OF ELIE WIESEL

Legends of Our Time. New York: Holt, Rinehart and Winston, 1968.

Night. New York: Avon Books, 1969.

One Generation After. New York: Random House, 1970.

A Jew Today. New York: Random House, 1978.

A Beggar in Jerusalem: A Novel. New York: Schocken, 1985.

The Six Days of Destruction: Meditations toward Hope. With Albert Friedlander. Mahwah, NJ: Paulist Press, 1988.

Twilight [1987]. New York: Warner Books, 1989.

A Journey of Faith. With John Cardinal O'Connor. New York: Donald I. Fine, 1990.

From the Kingdom of Memory: Reminiscences. New York: Summit, 1990.

All Rivers Run to the Sea: Memoirs. New York: Schocken, 1996.

And the Sea Is Never Full: Memoirs. New York: Alfred A. Knopf, 1999.

After the Darkness: Reflections on the Holocaust. New York: Schocken, 2002.

Night, Dawn, the Accident: A Trilogy [1972]. New York: Hill and Wang, 2004.

A Mad Desire to Dance: A Novel. New York: Alfred A. Knopf, 2009.

Open Heart. New York: Alfred A. Knopf, 2012.

Radu Ioanid is Director of the United States Holocaust Memorial Museum's International Archival Programs Division and author of several books on Romanian history and the Holocaust, including *The Holocaust in Romania: The Destruction of Jews and Gypsies under the Antonescu Regime, 1940–1944* and *The Ransom of the Jews: The Story of the Extraordinary Secret Bargain between Romania and Israel*. He earned his first doctorate at the University of Cluj, Romania, and his second doctorate at École des Hautes Études en Sciences Sociales, Paris, France. From 2003 to 2004, he served as the vice president for the International Commission on the Holocaust in Romania, chaired by Elie Wiesel. In 2006, Ioanid received the distinguished rank of Officier des Artes et des Lettres, conferred by the French minister of culture.

Peggy Frankston represents the United States Holocaust Memorial Museum in France.

Printed in the USA
CPSIA information can be obtained
at www.ICGtesting.com
LVHW040919040924
789805LV00034B/31

9 780253 045287